הִנְנִי

The New Hebrew Through Prayer

Script Writing Workbook

Roberta Osser Baum

Cover and Book Design: Itzhack Shelomi
Project Editor: Terry S. Kaye

Springfield, New Jersey
www.behrmanhouse.com
ISBN 978-0-87441-173-7
Manufactured in the United States of America

LESSON 1

שָׁלוֹם

Shin ש

Follow the arrows to write the letter.

Trace the letter.

Practice writing the letter.

Practice writing the letter and vowel.

Lamed ל ל

Follow the arrows to write the letter.

Trace the letter.

Practice writing the letter.

ל

Practice writing the word-part.

לָ

Vav | ו

Follow the arrow to write the letter.

Trace the letter.

Practice writing the letter.

Practice writing the vowel.

Practice writing the letter and vowel.

Practice writing the word-part.

Final Mem ם ם

Follow the arrows to write the letter.

ם

Trace the letter.

Practice writing the letter.

ם

Practice writing the word-part.

לוֹם

Practice writing the word.

שָׁלוֹם

Vocabulary Know-How

שָׁלוֹם means "peace," "hello," and "good-bye."

Write the following in script:

- the way you greet your friend ____________________
- the opposite of war ____________________

LESSON 2

LETTERS YOU KNOW: שׁ ל ו ם

שַׁבָּת

Bet בּ בּ

Follow the arrows to write the letter.

בּ בּ בּ בּ בּ בּ בּ בּ בּ בּ בּ בּ

Trace the letter.

בּ בּ בּ בּ בּ בּ בּ בּ בּ בּ בּ בּ

Practice writing the letter.

בּ

Practice writing the letter and vowel on each line.

בָּ

שַׁ

Practice writing the word-part.

שַׁבָּ

Tav ת ת   תּ תּ

Follow the arrows to write the letter.

Trace the letter.

Practice writing the letter on each line.

תּ

ת

Practice writing the letter and vowel on each line.

תּוֹ

תַּ

Practice writing the word on each line.

בַּת

שַׁבָּת

Practice writing the phrase.

שַׁבָּת שָׁלוֹם

Vocabulary Know-How

בַּת means "daughter."

Write the word בַּת in script to complete the phrase.

מִצְוָה ____________________

שַׁבָּת means "rest" and "the seventh day."

Write the following in script:

- the name of the day of rest ____________________
- the name of the seventh day ____________________
- the phrase we use to greet friends on שַׁבָּת ____________________

What is the English meaning of the phrase you wrote?

____

CONNECTIONS

Connect the matching letters.

ס   ל   ת   בּ

ל   ו   שׁ   ת

ו   ם   בּ   שׁ

WORD WIZ

Connect the matching words.

שַׁבָּת	בַּת
תַּם	שָׁלוֹם
שָׁלוֹם	שַׁבָּת
בַּת	תַּם

WHO AM I?

Write the answers to the questions below in script. You will find the answers in "Word Wiz."

1. I am my parents' daughter.
   Who am I? ______________________________

2. I am the seventh day of the week.
   Who am I? ______________________________

3. I mean "peace."
   Who am I? ______________________________

LESSON 3

LETTERS YOU KNOW: שׁ ל ו מ ב תּ ת

בְּרָכָה

Resh ר ר

Follow the arrow to write the letter.

ר

Trace the letter.

ר ר ר ר ר ר ר ר ר ר ר ר

Practice writing the letter.

ר

Practice writing the letter and vowel on each line.

רָ

בְּ

Practice writing the word-part.

בְּרָ

Chaf כ כ

Follow the arrow to write the letter.

כ

Trace the letter.

כ כ כ כ כ כ כ כ כ כ כ כ

Practice writing the letter.

כ

Practice writing the letter and vowel.

כָ

Practice writing the word-part.

כָכָ

NUMBER IT

Write the number of the print letter next to the matching script letter.

	Script	Print	
______	פּ	ר	.1
______	ל	ם	.2
______	ם	בּ	.3
______	ר	כ	.4
______	כ	ל	.5

Hay ה ה

Follow the arrows to write the letter.

ה ה ה ה ה ה ה ה ה ה ה ה

Trace the letter.

ה ה ה ה ה ה ה ה ה ה ה ה

Practice writing the letter.

ה

Practice writing the letter and vowel.

הוֹ

Practice writing the word-part.

כָה

Practice writing the word.

בְּרָכָה

Vocabulary Know-How

בְּרָכָה means "blessing."

בְּרָכוֹת means "blessings."

Both words are built on the root ברכ ("bless" or "praise").

Write the root in script. _____ _____ _____

Write the word for "blessing" in script. ____________________

Write the word for "blessings" in script. ____________________

Final Chaf ך

בָּרוּךְ

Trace the letter.

Follow the arrows to write the letter.

Practice writing the letter.

Practice writing the letter and vowel on each line.

Practice writing the vowel.

Practice writing the word-part on each line.

רוּךְ בָּרוּ

Practice writing the word.

בָּרוּךְ

WORD PLAY

Use script letters and vowels to write words that sound like English.

בּ ל וֹ תּ ר ת

boat ___________ toe ___________

row ___________ roll ___________

LETTERS YOU KNOW:
שׁ ל ו מ בּ תּ ת ר כ ה ק

אַתָּה

Alef א א

Trace the letter.

א א א א א א

Follow the arrows to write the letter.

א א א א א א

Practice writing the letter.

א

Practice writing the letter and vowel on each line.

אַ תָּ

Practice writing the word-part on each line.

אַתָּ

תָּה

Practice writing the word.

אַתָּה

BLESSING PHRASE

The phrase בָּרוּךְ אַתָּה means "Praised are You" or "Blessed are You."

Write the phrase in script. ______________________________

Yud י י

יְיָ

Follow the arrow to write the letter.

Trace the letter.

Practice writing the letter.

Practice writing the look-alike letter on each line.

Practice writing the word.

יְיָ

Practice writing the phrase.

אַתָּה יְיָ

BLESSING PHRASE

בָּרוּךְ אַתָּה יְיָ means "Praised are You, Adonai" or "Blessed are You, Adonai."

Write the phrase in script. ______________________________

Write the word that:

- is built on the root ברכ ___________________
- means "you" ___________________
- is a name for God ___________________

TIC-TAC-TOE

Write the matching script letters in the blank Tic-Tac-Toe grid.

Play both games with a friend.

Write X or O in each block when you read the letter correctly.

ך	ם	א
י	שׁ	ה
ר	כ	ל

NAME GAME

Write the script form of each letter above its name.

ו בּ ר ל ה שׁ א ם כ י ך ת

______	______	______	______	______	______
Lamed	Alef	Tav	Resh	Chaf	Yud
______	______	______	______	______	______
Final Mem	Bet	Hay	Vav	Final Chaf	Shin

Mem מ מ   מֶלֶךְ

Follow the arrows to write the letter.

מ מ מ מ מ מ מ מ מ מ מ מ

Trace the letter.

מ מ מ מ מ מ מ מ מ מ מ מ

Practice writing the letter.

מ

Practice writing the letter and vowel.

מֶ

Practice writing the word-part on each line.

מֶלֶ

לֶךְ

Practice writing the word.

מֶלֶךְ

BLESSING PHRASE

מֶלֶךְ means "ruler."

Write the missing word in script to complete the phrase below.

אֱלֹהֵינוּ __________ הָעוֹלָם

Now fill in the missing English word.

our God, __________ of the world

LESSON 5

LETTERS YOU KNOW:

שׁ ל ו ס ב תּ ת ר
כ ה ק א י מ

שְׁמַע יִשְׂרָאֵל

Ayin ע ע

Follow the arrow to write the letter.

ע ע ע ע ע ע ע ע ע ע ע ע

Trace the letter.

ע ע ע ע ע ע ע ע ע ע ע ע

Practice writing the letter.

ע

Practice writing the word-part on each line.

שְׁמַ

מַע

Practice writing the word on each line.

שְׁמַע

הָעוֹלָם

לִשְׁמֹעַ

Sin שׂ שׂ

Follow the arrows to write the letter.

שׂ שׂ שׂ שׂ שׂ שׂ שׂ שׂ שׂ שׂ שׂ שׂ

Practice writing the letter on each line.

שׂ

שׂ

Practice writing the word-part on each line.

יִשְׂ

רָאֵל

Practice writing the word or phrase on each line.

יִשְׂרָאֵל

שָׂרָה

עֹשֵׂה שָׁלוֹם

Vocabulary Know-How

שְׁמַע יִשְׂרָאֵל means "Hear, O Israel."

Write the following in script:

- the word calling us to hear ____________________
- the word meaning the Jewish people ____________________

Nun נ נ

יְיָ אֱלֹהֵינוּ

Follow the arrow to write the letter.

נ

Trace the letter.

Practice writing the letter.

נ

Practice writing the word-part on each line.

אֱלֹ

הֵינוּ

Practice writing the word on each line.

אֱלֹהֵינוּ

עָלֵינוּ

שְׁכִינָה

Vocabulary Know-How

יְיָ אֱלֹהֵינוּ means "Adonai our God".

Write the phrase in script. ____________________

Write the sentence in script.

בָּרוּךְ אַתָּה, יְיָ אֱלֹהֵינוּ, מֶלֶךְ הָעוֹלָם

____

Praised are You, Adonai our God, Ruler of the world

WORD REVIEW

Write each word in script three times.

שָׁלוֹם ____________ ____________ ____________

שַׁבָּת ____________ ____________ ____________

בְּרָכָה ____________ ____________ ____________

SILENT PARTNER

One letter in each pair below makes a sound; the other does not. In script, write the letter that makes a sound.

1. תּ א ______
2. ע בּ ______
3. ו ע ______
4. שׁ ע ______
5. א ךְ ______
6. מ ע ______
7. א ר ______
8. שׁ ע ______
9. ל א ______

In script, write the two letters that do not make a sound. ______ ______

Ḥet ח ח   יְיָ אֶחָד

Follow the arrows to write the letter.

ח ח ח ח ח ח ח ח ח ח ח ח

Trace the letter.

ח ח ח ח ח ח ח ח ח ח ח ח

Practice writing the letter.

ח

Practice writing the word-part.

כֶחָ

Practice writing the word on each line.

חַלָּה

כַחַת

מִנְחָה

CONNECTIONS

Connect the matching letters.

ת	ה
ח	ת
ה	ח

ס	ע
א	א
כ	ם

ו	י
נ	נ
י	ו

Dalet ד ד

Follow the arrows to write the letter.

ד ד ד ד ד ד ד ד ד ד ד ד

Trace the letter.

ד ד ד ד ד ד ד ד ד ד ד ד

Practice writing the letter.

ד

Practice writing the word-part.

חָד

Practice writing the word or phrase on each line.

אֶחָד

דִינָה

לְעוֹלָם וָעֶד

Vocabulary Know-How

יְיָ אֶחָד means "Adonai is One."

Write the phrase in script. ____________________

Write the prayer in script.

שְׁמַע יִשְׂרָאֵל, יְיָ אֱלֹהֵינוּ, יְיָ אֶחָד.

____

Hear O Israel, Adonai is our God, Adonai is One.

LESSON 6

LETTERS YOU KNOW:

שׁ ל ו ם בּ תּ ת ר כ ה
ק א י מ ע שׂ נ ח ד

אַבְרָהָם
שָׂרָה

Vet ב ב

Follow the arrow to write the letter.

ב ב ב ב ב ב ב ב ב ב ב ב

Practice writing the letter.

ב

Practice writing the word-part on each line.

אַבְ

רָהָם

Practice writing the word on each line.

אַבְרָהָם

הַבְדָּלָה

וְאָהַבְתָּ

OUR PATRIARCHS

Connect the Hebrew name of each patriarch to the matching English.

Abraham	יַעֲקֹב
Isaac	אַבְרָהָם
Jacob	יִצְחָק

Write the missing name in script on the line below.

________________, יִצְחָק, יַעֲקֹב

PRAYER PHRASES

Write each phrase in script.

1. וְאָהַבְתָּ אֵת יְיָ אֱלֹהֶיךָ

____

2. אֱלֹהֵינוּ וֵאלֹהֵי אֲבוֹתֵינוּ אֱלֹהֵי אַבְרָהָם

____

3. עַל יַד נְבִיאֶךָ

____

4. בְּכָל עֵת וּבְכָל שָׁעָה בִּשְׁלוֹמֶךָ

____

Koof ק ק

Follow the arrows to write the letter.

ק ק ק ק ק ק ק ק ק ק ק ק

Trace the letter.

ק ק ק ק ק ק ק ק ק ק ק ק

Practice writing the letter.

ק

Practice writing the word-part on each line.

רִבְ יַעֲ

קָה קֹב

Practice writing the word on each line.

רִבְקָה יַעֲקֹב

OUR MATRIARCHS

Connect the Hebrew name of each matriarch to the matching English.

Sarah	רָחֵל
Rebecca	לֵאָה
Leah	שָׂרָה
Rachel	רִבְקָה

Tsadee צ צ

Follow the arrows to write the letter.

Trace the letter.

Practice writing the letter.

Practice writing the word or phrase on each line.

יִצְחָק

בֵּיצִית

הַמּוֹצִיא לֶחֶם

מִצְוָה

BLESSING BEE

Complete the blessing phrase in script.

______ מִן הָאָרֶץ

who brings forth bread from the earth

OUR ANCESTORS

Write the names of the patriarchs and matriarchs in script.

אַבְרָהָם ______ שָׂרָה ______ יִצְחָק ______ רִבְקָה ______

יַעֲקֹב ______ לֵאָה ______ רָחֵל ______

LETTER PRACTICE

Below are the names of the letters you have learned to write in script so far.
Write each script letter above its name.

Mem	Vav	Lamed	Resh	Hay
Tsadee	Chaf	Nun	Tav	Vet
Sin	Final Mem	Ayin	Bet	Yud
Alef	Shin	Final Chaf	Dalet	Ḥet
				Koof

Which two letters form the name of the Hebrew alphabet? ______ ______

CANDLELIGHTING

Write in script the blessing we recite when we light Shabbat candles.

בָּרוּךְ אַתָּה יְיָ אֱלֹהֵינוּ מֶלֶךְ הָעוֹלָם

____

אֲשֶׁר קִדְּשָׁנוּ בְּמִצְוֹתָיו וְצִוָּנוּ

____

לְהַדְלִיק נֵר שֶׁל שַׁבָּת.

____

PRAYER POWER

Write in script the name of each blessing, prayer, and song below.

1. יוֹצֵר אוֹר _______________
2. קַדִּישׁ _______________
3. הַתִּקְוָה _______________
4. מַעֲרִיב עֲרָבִים _______________
5. קִדּוּשׁ _______________
6. עֲבוֹדָה _______________
7. בְּרָכוֹת שֶׁל מִצְוָה _______________

Write the name of Israel's national anthem in script. _______________

LESSON 7

LETTERS YOU KNOW:

שׁ ל ו ם בּ תּ ת ר כ ה ק
א י מ ע שׂ נ ח ד ב ק צ

תְּפִלָּה

Fay פ פּ

Follow the arrow to write the letter.

פּ פּ פּ פּ פּ פּ פּ פּ פּ פּ פּ פּ

Trace the letter.

פּ פּ פּ פּ פּ פּ פּ פּ פּ פּ פּ פּ

Practice writing the letter.

פּ

Practice writing the word-part on each line.

תְּפִ

פִּלָּה

Write the word on each line.

תְּפִלָּה

שׁוֹפָר

נֶפֶשׁ

VOCABULARY KNOW-HOW

תְּפִלָּה means "prayer."

תְּפִלָּה is another name for the עֲמִידָה—the group of blessings at the heart of every prayer service. The עֲמִידָה is also known as the שְׁמוֹנֶה עֶשְׂרֵה.

Write the three names here.

_______________ _______________ _______________

FROM THE תְּפִלָּה

Write the prayer phrases below in script.

1. אֲדֹנָי שְׂפָתַי תִּפְתָּח

____

2. וְרוֹפֵא חוֹלִים

____

3. וּמְקַיֵּם אֱמוּנָתוֹ לִישֵׁנֵי עָפָר

____

4. וּבַיּוֹם הַשְּׁבִיעִי שָׁבַת וַיִּנָּפַשׁ

____

5. וּתְפִלָּתָם בְּאַהֲבָה תְקַבֵּל

____

Tet ט ט — הַפְטָרָה

Follow the arrows to write the letter.

ט ט ט ט ט ט ט ט ט ט ט ט

Trace the letter.

ט ט ט ט ט ט ט ט ט ט ט ט

Practice writing the letter.

ט

Practice writing the word-part on each line.

הַפְ

טָרָה

Practice writing the word or phrase on each line.

הַפְטָרָה

טַלִית

יוֹם טוֹב

טֵבֵת

Vocabulary Know-How

At the conclusion of the Torah reading on Shabbat and holidays, an honored person in the congregation reads a section from Prophets called the הַפְטָרָה ("conclusion"). The haftarah is related thematically to that week's Torah portion or to a holiday season.

Write the word הַפְטָרָה in script. ____________________

NAME A PROPHET

Write the name of each prophet below in script.

Isaiah	יְשַׁעְיָהוּ	____________________
Jeremiah	יִרְמְיָהוּ	____________________
Jonah	יוֹנָה	____________________
Habakkuk	חֲבַקּוּק	____________________
Zephaniah	צְפַנְיָה	____________________
Malachi	מַלְאָכִי	____________________

WORD PLAY

Use Hebrew letters and vowels to write words that sound like English.

food ______________ tool ______________ lake ______________

meat ______________ name ______________ feet ______________

Zayin ז ז

מְזוּזָה

Follow the arrows to write the letter.

ז ז ז ז ז ז ז ז ז ז ז ז ז

Trace the letter.

ז ז ז ז ז ז ז ז ז ז ז ז ז

Practice writing the letter.

ז

Practice writing the word-part on each line.

מְזוּ

זָה

Practice writing the word or phrase on each line.

מְזוּזָה

מַזָּל טוֹב

מַחֲזוֹר

זְרוֹעַ

A SOUND SLEEPER

Write the script form of each letter below.

Read the sounds aloud to hear a sound sleeper.

שׁ ז שׁ צ ז צ ז

Vocabulary Know-How

מְזוּזָה means "doorpost."

We place a מְזוּזָה on the doorposts of our homes to remind us to follow God's commandments.

PRAYER PHRASES

Write this sentence from the conclusion of וְאָהַבְתָּ.

וּכְתַבְתָּם עַל מְזֻזוֹת בֵּיתֶךָ וּבִשְׁעָרֶיךָ.

Write them on the doorposts of your house and on your gates.

Now practice writing these sentences from the beginning of וְאָהַבְתָּ.

וְאָהַבְתָּ אֵת יְיָ אֱלֹהֶיךָ

בְּכָל לְבָבְךָ וּבְכָל נַפְשְׁךָ וּבְכָל מְאֹדֶךָ

וְהָיוּ הַדְּבָרִים הָאֵלֶּה, אֲשֶׁר אָנֹכִי מְצַוְּךָ הַיּוֹם,
עַל לְבָבֶךָ

LETTERS YOU KNOW:

שׁ ל ו ם בּ תּ ת ר כ ה ה ב א י

מ ע שׂ נ ח ד ב ק ז פ ט כ

סֻכּוֹת

Samech ס ס

Follow the arrows to write the letter.

ס ס ס ס ס ס ס ס ס ס ס ס

Trace the letter.

ס ס ס ס ס ס ס ס ס ס ס ס

Practice writing the letter.

ס

Practice writing the letter and vowel on each line.

סֻ סוֹ

Practice writing the word-part on each line.

סֹק סִים

Practice writing the word on each line.

לַעֲסֹק

נִסִים

Kaf כּ כּ

Follow the arrows to write the letter.

כּ כּ כּ כּ כּ כּ כּ כּ כּ כּ כּ כּ

Practice writing the letter on each line.

כּ

כ

ך

Practice writing the word-part on each line.

סֻכּוֹ

כּוֹת

Practice writing the word on each line.

סֻכּוֹת

כְּנֶסֶת

כָּמֹכָה

סוֹמֵךְ

Vocabulary Know-How

סֻכּוֹת means "booths" or "shelters."

Read the following sentence from the הַשְׁכִּיבֵנוּ prayer in which we ask God to "spread over us the shelter of Your peace."

וּפְרוֹשׂ עָלֵינוּ סֻכַּת שְׁלוֹמֶךָ.

Now write the sentence in script.

____

Which phrase means "shelter of Your peace"? ____________________

SOUNDS LIKE

Connect the sound-alike letters.

ת	כּ
ק	ב
ו	ט
כ	שׂ
ס	ח

Write each pair of sound-alike letters next to their sound.

K _____ _____ **T** _____ _____ **S** _____ _____ **Ḥ** _____ _____ **V** _____ _____

CELEBRATING SUKKOT

Write in script the ending of the blessing we say when:

- we sit in the sukkah:

לֵישֵׁב בַּסֻּכָּה ______________________

- we shake the lulav:

עַל נְטִילַת לוּלָב ______________________

Pay פּ פּ   פֶּסַח

Follow the arrows to write the letter.

פּ פּ פּ פּ פּ פּ פּ פּ פּ פּ פּ פּ

Practice writing the letter on each line.

פּ פּ

Practice writing the word-part on each line.

פֶּסַ סַח

Practice writing the word on each line.

פֶּסַח

פָּרָשָׁה

כִּפָּה

SEDER PLATE

Write the names of the items on the seder plate in script.

מָרוֹר כַּרְפַּס בֵּיצָה

מַצָּה זְרוֹעַ חֲרוֹסֶת

Which item reminds us of the Israelites' bitter lives in slavery? ________________

PICTIONARY

Write the names of the holidays below in script.
Then draw a picture of an object that represents the holiday; for example, a gragger for Purim.

DRAW	HOLIDAY	WRITE
	רֹאשׁ הַשָּׁנָה	______________
	יוֹם כִּפּוּר	______________
	סֻכּוֹת	______________
	שִׂמְחַת תּוֹרָה	______________
	חֲנֻכָּה	______________
	פּוּרִים	______________
	פֶּסַח	______________
	שָׁבוּעוֹת	______________

Final Fay ף

קְלָף

Follow the arrows to write the letter.

Trace the letter.

Practice writing the word-part. לָף

Practice writing the letter. ף

Practice writing the word on each line.

קְלָף

חֹרֶף

יוֹסֵף

Vocabulary Know-How

The Hebrew word for "parchment" is קְלָף.
קְלָף is the treated skin from a kosher animal.
The סֵפֶר תּוֹרָה and the scroll inside a מְזוּזָה are written on קְלָף.

Write the following Hebrew words in script:

- our holiest book ____________________
- parchment ____________________
- the object we hang on our doorposts ____________________

LETTERS YOU KNOW:

שׁ ל ו ם בּ תּ ת ר כ ה ק א י מ ע

שׂ נ ח ד ב ק ז פ ט ך ס כּ פּ ף

מָגֵן

Gimmel ג ג

Follow the arrows to write the letter.

ג ג ג ג ג ג ג ג ג ג ג ג

Trace the letter.

ג ג ג ג ג ג ג ג ג ג ג ג

Practice writing the letter.

ג

Practice writing the letter and vowel.

גֵ

Practice writing the word-part on each line.

מְגִ גִים

Practice writing the word on each line.

מְגִלָּה

חֲגִים

עֹנֶג

Final Nun | ן

Follow the arrow to write the letter.

ן

Trace the letter.

Practice writing the letter.

ן

Practice writing the look-alike letters.

י ו ן

Practice writing the word-part on each line.

אָמֵ   מֵן

Practice writing the word on each line.

אָמֵן

הַגָּפֶן

צִיוֹן

SCRAMBLED WORDS

Unscramble the words and write the ending for the blessing over wine.

פְּרִי   בּוֹרֵא   הַגָּפֶן

Vocabulary Know-How

מָגֵן means "shield."

מָגֵן דָּוִד means "shield of David." Write the phrase in script.

____

מָגֵן אַבְרָהָם means "shield of Abraham." Write the phrase in script.

____

Add the words בָּרוּךְ אַתָּה יְיָ before each of the four haftarah blessing endings below.

הָאֵל הַנֶּאֱמָן בְּכָל דְּבָרָיו. ______________________

מְשַׂמֵּחַ צִיּוֹן בְּבָנֶיהָ. ______________________

מָגֵן דָּוִד. ______________________

מְקַדֵּשׁ הַשַּׁבָּת. ______________________

MY HEBREW DICTIONARY

מִלּוֹן means "dictionary." Write the word מִלּוֹן in script. ____________________

Write each Hebrew word in script next to the matching English word below.

שׁוֹפָר מַצָּה כִּפָּה טַלִּית צְדָקָה מְזוּזָה

מִצְוָה חַלָּה הַבְדָּלָה תּוֹרָה סֻכָּה מְגִלָּה

Torah ______________ mitzvah ______________ ḥallah ______________

kippah ______________ tallit ______________ sukkah ______________

megillah ______________ tzedakah ______________ mezuzah ______________

shofar ______________ matzah ______________ havdalah ______________

Final Tsadee ץ ץ   אֶרֶץ, אָרֶץ

Trace the letter.

ץ ץ ץ ץ ץ ץ ץ ץ

Follow the arrows to write the letter.

ץ ץ ץ ץ ץ ץ ץ ץ

Practice writing the letter.

ץ

Practice writing the word-part.

אָרֶ

אֶרֶ

רֶץ

Practice writing the word on each line.

אָרֶץ

אֶרֶץ

עֵץ

SCRAMBLED WORDS

Unscramble the words and write the ending for the blessing over fruit.

הָעֵץ פְּרִי בּוֹרֵא

Unscramble the words and write the ending for the blessing over bread.

מִן הַמּוֹצִיא הָאָרֶץ לֶחֶם

VOCABULARY KNOW-HOW

אֶרֶץ and אָרֶץ mean "land."

The land of Israel is known as אֶרֶץ יִשְׂרָאֵל.

Write the phrase in script. ____________________

Write the names of these cities and places in אֶרֶץ יִשְׂרָאֵל.

תֵּל־אָבִיב	נֶגֶב	צְפַת	יְרוּשָׁלַיִם
________	________	________	________
גָּלִיל	מְצָדָה	גּוֹלָן	חֵיפָה
________	________	________	________

LOOKS LIKE

Write the Hebrew letter for each letter name below.

____	____	____	____	____
Gimmel	Yud	Zayin	Final Nun	Vav
____	____	____	____	____
Lamed	Final Fay	Koof	Final Tsadee	Final Chaf

FAMILY CONNECTIONS

Connect the family letters.

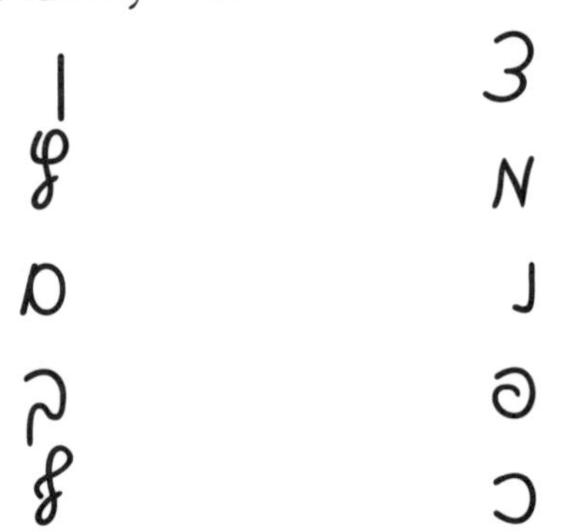

ALEF-BET REVIEW

Write the letters of the Hebrew alphabet in script.

א

בּ

ב

ג

ד

ה

ו

ז

ח

ט

י

כּ

כ

ך

ל

מ

ם

נ

ן

ס

ע

פּ

פ

ף

צ

ץ

ק

ר

שׁ

שׂ

תּ

ת

WRAP-UP

Write the prayer phrases in script.

1. וְזֹאת הַתּוֹרָה אֲשֶׁר שָׂם מֹשֶׁה

2. וְהָיוּ לְטֹטָפֹת בֵּין עֵינֶיךָ

3. זֵכֶר לִיצִיאַת מִצְרָיִם

4. מְכַלְכֵּל חַיִּים בְּחֶסֶד

5. יָאֵר יְיָ פָּנָיו אֵלֶיךָ וִיחֻנֶּךָּ

6. כִּי מִצִּיּוֹן תֵּצֵא תוֹרָה

7. מְלֹא כָל הָאָרֶץ כְּבוֹדוֹ

8. הַמַּבְדִּיל בֵּין קֹדֶשׁ לְחוֹל

9. וּבְמִצְוֹתֶיךָ תִּרְדּוֹף נַפְשִׁי

10. שֶׁהֶחֱיָנוּ וְקִיְּמָנוּ וְהִגִּיעָנוּ